Central & Southern Essex
Edited by Lynsey Hawkins

Young Writers

First published in Great Britain in 2007 by:
Young Writers
Remus House
Coltsfoot Drive
Peterborough
PE2 9JX
Telephone: 01733 890066
Website: www.youngwriters.co.uk

All Rights Reserved

© Copyright Contributors 2007

SB ISBN 978-1 84602 955 4

Foreword

Young Writers was established in 1991 and has been passionately devoted to the promotion of reading and writing in children and young adults ever since. The quest continues today. Young Writers remains as committed to the nurturing of poetic and literary talent as ever.

This year's Young Writers competition has proven as vibrant and dynamic as ever and we are delighted to present a showcase of the best poetry from across the UK and in some cases overseas. Each poem has been selected from a wealth of *Little Laureates* entries before ultimately being published in this, our sixteenth primary school poetry series.

Once again, we have been supremely impressed by the overall quality of the entries we have received. The imagination, energy and creativity which has gone into each young writer's entry made choosing the poems a challenging and often difficult but ultimately hugely rewarding task - the general high standard of the work submitted ensured this opportunity to bring their poetry to a larger appreciative audience.

We sincerely hope you are pleased with this final collection and that you will enjoy *Little Laureates Central & Southern Essex* for many years to come.

Contents

Baddow Hall Junior School

Molly Harris (10)	1
Lauren Clarke (8)	2
Charlotte Broad (10)	3
Kiera Cousins (9)	4
Matthew Brown (9)	5
Jack Hanby (7)	6
Molly Robinson (8)	7
Poppy Johnson (7)	8
Katie Vale (7)	9
Joseph Kiff (7)	10
Emma Levis (8)	11
Joseph Hunt (7)	12
Jamie Smith (7)	13
Luke Egleton (8)	14
Jamie Matthews (9)	15
Emily Morrow (9)	16
Roisin O'Hagan (8)	17
Matilda Wanless (8)	18
Rebecca Drage (8)	19
Sam Bellman (9)	20
Emily Strudwick (10)	21
Lewis Joslin (11)	22
William Watt (11)	23
Samuel Newsome & Joe Land (9)	24
Sarah Austin (9)	25
Jodie Ridgewell Wright (8)	26
Hannah Gridley (9)	27
Amber Spencer (9)	28
George Shaw (11)	29
Lucy Peckham (10)	30
Kelsey Fisher (10)	31
Hannah Newsome (8)	32
Alicia Benham (8)	33
Nathan Brearley (8)	34

Darlinghurst Primary School

Bradley Moody (10)	35
Sarah Nash (9)	36

Danial Nash (9)   37
Jarel Jack (9)   38
Haleema Khatun (9)   39
Thomas Wright (8)   40
Joshua Fix (8)   41
Owen Lee Burton (8)   42
Charlotte Tanner (9)   43
Jamie Cooper (9)   44
Kai Davies (8)   45
Edward Mukudu (9)   46
Lucie Wade (9)   47
Nathan Woollard (9)   48
George Sadler (8)   49
Max Cottage (8)   50

Fairways Primary School

Olivia Inskip-Hickey (9)   51
Lauren Jefferies (10)   52
Amanda Bowers (10)   53
Anna Lawrance (10)   54
Bethany Kiamil (11)   55
Daniel Lewis (11)   56
Rachel Morris (10)   57
Owain Tomlin (10)   58
Iwan Tomlin (8)   59
Jessica Bunting (8)   60
Hollie Zucker (7)   61
Kate Ridley (7)   62
Zoe Bolton-Smith (11)   63
Léoni Hughes (10)   64
Tara Said (9)   65
Chloe Denby (8)   66
Jade Shaw (9)   67
Jessica-May Davey (8)   68
Megan Preece (9)   69
Georgia Stoneham (9)   70

Great Waltham CE Primary School

Becky Thwaites (10)   71
Reece Field (10)   72
Robert Green (10)   73

Bethan Culling (11)	74
Cameron Worcester (10)	75
Catherine Warner (11)	76
Josie Coventry (11)	77
Jenny Armstrong (10)	78
Daniel Andrews (11)	79
Matty Read & Joshua De'ath (10)	80
Elsie Hayes (9)	81
Thomas Strangwige (10)	82
Samuel Tyler (10)	83
Victoria Hawes (11)	84
George Martin (9)	85
Victoria Seymour (11)	86
George Dodd (9)	87
Morgan Gentry (10)	88

St John's CE Primary School, Danbury

Holly Hawkins (11)	89
Stephanie Ovenden (10)	90
Conner Austin (10)	91
Lewis Simmons (10)	92
Mark Bandell (11)	93
Joshua Warner (11)	94
Stuart Allen (10)	95
Megan Obeney (9)	96
Samuel Rye (10)	97
Max Harding (9)	98
Hannah Norris (10)	99
Sophie Huntley (10)	100
Michael Boyd (9)	101
Joshua Crowe (8)	102
Andrew Smiley (8)	103
Amelia Western (9)	104
Rebecca Manning (10)	105
Sean Madle (9)	106
Thomas Braben (10)	107
Andrew Hariz (9)	108
Fern Gossett (10)	109
Heather Dorrell (9)	110
Joe O'Sullivan (9)	111
Adam Knights (9)	112

Chantelle Haley (9) — 113
Felix Flechtner (10) — 114
Rebecca Perkins (10) — 115
Nicholas Perkins (9) — 116

The Daiglen School
Edward Dowling (9) — 117
Samuel Apata (9) — 118
Joseph Klein (8) — 119
Harry Osborn (8) — 120
Jack Jenkins (9) — 121
Max Rabey (8) — 122
Peter Piskov (8) — 123
Nana Kwasi Dartey-Baah Jnr (8) — 124
Eddie Williams (7) — 125
Zachary Cannon (7) — 126
Miles Barella (10) — 127
Louis Hart (10) — 128
Alex Minkey (9) — 129
Jack Sansom (9) — 130
George Jamieson (9) — 131
Joshua Butt (10) — 132
Onur Sevigen (10) — 133
Lewis Woollard (7) — 134
Max Goreham (10) — 135
James Wright (10) — 136
Eren Sadik (11) — 137
Jaikaram Sandhu (11) — 138
Garth Jones (9) — 139
Samuel Meah (10) — 140
Saurav Prabhakar (10) — 141
Harrison Jones (10) — 142
Ryan Williams (8) — 143
Zachary Cohen (8) — 144
Charlie Wright (8) — 145
Damien Zimelstern (11) — 146

Westborough Primary School
Jasmine Samson (7) — 147
William Semple (8) — 148

Ashleigh Gill (8)	149
Jasper Huxtable (9)	150
Thomas Parker (9)	151
Ben Crawford (10)	152
Thom Amar (10)	153
Robin Tidd (10)	154
Daisy Appleton (9)	155
Mollie Fryer (10)	156
Liam Davis (10)	157
Danielle Jefferies (9)	158
Rochana Reeves (9)	159
Alexia Parks (10)	160
Sophia Shaw (9)	161
Jessica Lynch (8)	162
Eureka Zaman (11)	163
Maddie Davies (10)	164
Chad Davies (11)	165
Isaac Smith (11)	166
Rhys Masterson (10)	167
Lewis Sturley (11)	168
Victoria Chinery (10)	169
Kieran Burns (11)	170
Amin Babar (10)	171
Klevin Demo (11)	172
Shannon Dorrington (11)	173
Hannah-Louise Hill (11)	174
Rachel Ellis (10)	175
Joe Hodges (11)	176
Lucy Urquhart (10)	177
Raihan Uddin (11)	178
Jade Atkin (10)	179
Alex Fowler (11)	180
Rebecca Cutmore (10)	181
Sophie Goddard (10)	182
Justin Davis (10)	183
Victoria Johnson (10)	184
Danielle Ford (11)	185
Ellie-Marie Shuff (10)	186
Maisie Davies (9)	187
Jordan Chandler (10)	188
Anitta Abraham (10)	189

Tasha Russell (10)	190
Jack Whitehead (10)	191
Helena Layzell (11)	192
Eunice Rutendo Mushonga (10)	193

The Poems

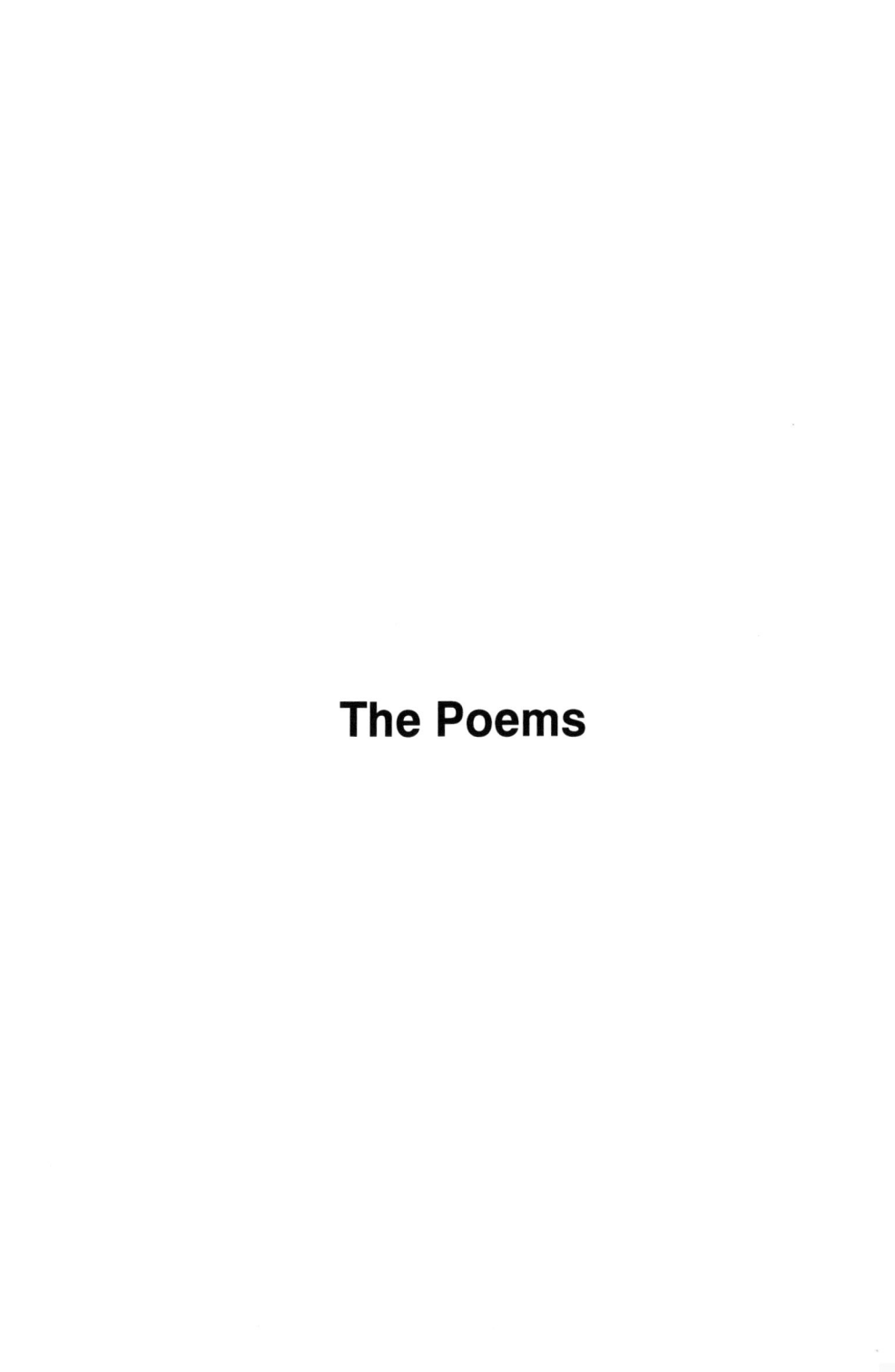

Best Friends

B est friends stay together all the time
E verybody has friends, they're all mine
S pecial friends are really kind
T hey share the same mind

F un in the playground
R unning around
I ndoors and outdoors equally found
E veryone playing
N ever falling out
D oing games together
S ome friends, you never doubt.

Molly Harris (10)
Baddow Hall Junior School

Birthday Girl

Today is my birthday
My friends are coming round
There's one million presents all to be found
All gather up and come round mine today
We're going to have fun, hip hip hooray
So let's blow out the candles and have a bit of cake
How many candles, there are eight
'Have a nice birthday,' everyone said
They filled up their bellies, happily fed
It's the end of the day; I don't want it to be over
I got a ride round town in a Land Rover
I can't wait until next year
When my birthday is near.

Lauren Clarke (8)
Baddow Hall Junior School

Dogs Are Cute

D ogs are always fun to play with
O ver cats, I love and prefer dogs
G uard dogs always keep you safe
S ome dogs can do clever tricks, so three cheers for dogs

A ll dogs are good to be with
R obbers can never escape with dogs guarding the house
E verybody should love and cherish dogs

C ute are dogs, always
U nder the table I find my sock, guess who? Yes, the dog
T ake a chance and get a dog
E very type of dog, I just love them all.

Charlotte Broad (10)
Baddow Hall Junior School

My Cat In The Snow

I have a cat and her name is Mia
She likes playing in the snow
I have another cat called Gaby
She seems to grow and grow.
I have two kittens
One called Midnight and the other is called Beauty
Some nights their eyes and whiskers glow.

One snowy morning Gaby and Mia were stuck outside in the snow
I opened the door and carried them in
I put them on the sofa and put a blanket over them
Later on in the day the kittens came running to their mum
Soon they were all tucked up in the blanket on the sofa
And then they all fell asleep
I sat next to them with my bag next to me
And then I started to read my book
It is really fun having cats and kittens
Because they are really playful.

Kiera Cousins (9)
Baddow Hall Junior School

My PS2

My PS2 is always freezing
And it gets me flaming
It will be the death of me some day
But for now I will just play.

When I play, my anger just blows away
And when I have a fight with my brother
I just go on my PS2
I play my favourite games and anger blows away.

And when I have finished
My tension and anger just go out of the window
It's my favourite thing ever.

Matthew Brown (9)
Baddow Hall Junior School

The Football Match

The pitch is as green as the sea
The ball is as round as the sun
They kick like a rock
The cheer is as loud as a storm
The players are as wild as a lion
The ref is a bossy boots.

Jack Hanby (7)
Baddow Hall Junior School

Winter

Cold icy winter sliding on the ice
Someone over there is building a snowman
Not many days until Christmas Day
Snowman has a carrot nose and a smiley mouth
Coal for some buttons and sticks for the arms
Everyone has fun at Christmas time.

Molly Robinson (8)
Baddow Hall Junior School

Clouds

As I look in the sky I see
A bird, a butterfly and a bumblebee
Even if they are white, they look so real
And now I can even see a seal!
When I go to bed I lose
The seal and a pair of shoes
When next morn I look in the sky, I see
A bird, a butterfly and a bumblebee!

Poppy Johnson (7)
Baddow Hall Junior School

My School

S mall writing is OK, if it is neat
C ool playtime is great if there is no heat
H ailstones are fun in the playground
O pening and reading books
O utside we have fun
L earning is fun, I get so much done.

Katie Vale (7)
Baddow Hall Junior School

Days Of The Week

Monday is black
Tuesday, sorry I am sacked
Wednesday I hate
Thursday is great
Friday I like because it is the end of school
Saturday I go to the Big Wall
Sunday I think is glum
Because I look so dumb.

Joseph Kiff (7)
Baddow Hall Junior School

The Week

Monday is a fun day
Tuesday is a blue day
Wednesdays are friends' days
Thursdays are our mothers' days
Friday is my own day
Saturday's a shatter day
Sunday's also fun day, the play day the May Day
So here is the week for you
Everyone has a favourite, *so choose!*

Emma Levis (8)
Baddow Hall Junior School

The Weather

The weather is hot, the weather is cold
Sometimes I think the weather is mould
Some days the weather is sunny
Some days it is runny
Some days it pours and never stops
Sometimes, one minute raining
The next minute not!
Sometimes the weather makes me feel relaxed
Sometimes it makes me feel worried
A sunset looks beautiful
Storms look ugly and make me feel sad.

Joseph Hunt (7)
Baddow Hall Junior School

Cars

A Ferrari is a sports car
A Mercedes goes far
Formula 1 cars get battered and bruised
Go-karts are fun
I'm driving in one soon
It's the end of the day
And it's time to have a rest
Dreaming of my cars
And see which one's the best.

Jamie Smith (7)
Baddow Hall Junior School

Drums

I play high tom on Monday
I play bass on Tuesday
On Wednesday I play snare
I like playing drums.

On Thursday I play cymbals
On Friday I play hi hats
On Saturday I play low tom
On Sunday I play all of them
I like playing drums.

Luke Egleton (8)
Baddow Hall Junior School

Dinosaurs

D inosaurs so big, so strong
I n the jungle, so fierce
N o man can stop them when they go
O h so big
S o really strong
A nd so big on the dance floor
U sed to rule but now dead
R eally so scary
   You would not want to dance with one.

Jamie Matthews (9)
Baddow Hall Junior School

When I See

When I see a dog, I always think
What is its name?
Where does it live?
Who owns it?

Then I see two dogs I think again
Do they get on? It looks like it!

The next day I walk home from school
I see a dog chasing a cat, why? I think
Then I realise that the dog must not like the cat.

I tell my mum I have never seen them before
My mum says they must be new
Perhaps some new people have moved in
There might be a friend for you!

Maybe they will start in my school
Wouldn't that be cool
Then we could walk to the park together
With our dogs and play the fool!

Emily Morrow (9)
Baddow Hall Junior School

Cats

Cats are furry
Cats are fat
Cats are lazy
Just like a rat
Cats are greedy
Cats are great
Everyone likes them
Even my mate
Cats purr
Cats play
Cats sleep every day.

Roisin O'Hagan (8)
Baddow Hall Junior School

My Dog

My soppy dog called Poppy
Is mad and very cocky
When I come home from school
She is always there for me
I stride with pride when I take her out
She is the best pet in the world.

Matilda Wanless (8)
Baddow Hall Junior School

Animals

Animals are the past and future
They make nature green and fresh
They make you wake up on a brand new day
If you look outside
You will see the pride
Cows say, 'Moo.'
So don't disturb them
And they won't disturb you.

Rebecca Drage (8)
Baddow Hall Junior School

The First Day With My Cat

The first day with my cat
He was cool and funny and fat
Every day I woke up, he was miaowing at a rat.

At breakfast he jumped up, miaowing as loud as he could
So I gave him a bit of my meat
But he wanted a bit of my pud.

After school I went through the door
He jumped up like crazy and I really wanted more
After his dinner, he didn't look that much thinner
At bedtime I said, 'My cat's a winner!'

Sam Bellman (9)
Baddow Hall Junior School

Happyness Spelt Wrong

Me, I am so happy
But my friends they aren't so lucky
My friends are really funny
Even though they don't have money.

My mum and dad are kind
Even though they have a lot on their mind
I wish that they had a better life
Instead of all the strife.

Emily Strudwick (10)
Baddow Hall Junior School

Jewels

All jewels are precious, here are a few of them:
D iamonds, sparkling in the light with dazzling brightness
I magine everything made of jewellery, absolutely beautiful
A methysts, luxurious, they always brighten your day
M arvellous emeralds, shining as green as the grass
O pals as milky white as the stars
N ecklaces made of jewels encrusted with platinum
D azzling rubies as red as the lava in a volcano
S apphires as blue as the breathtaking blue skies!

Lewis Joslin (11)
Baddow Hall Junior School

The Pigsty

Pigs standing up
Pigs falling down
Oinking to each other in a strange language
Bundling into their hedge
Forming a strange-shaped wedge
Ramming with their feet
To keep with the beat.

The farmer came out to see the commotion
Then he jumped as a pig tried to ram him
In a funny-looking motion
He closed the gate as a fat pig tried to escape
It hit the pig's head as he rolled in the mud
Then he stood up and landed with a thud
That was the end of poor little pig
All the others were happy and did a merry jig!

William Watt (11)
Baddow Hall Junior School

The Natural World, Wow!

Lava is red
Covering rock
Ash overhead
It makes the world rock

Spitting fire
Like it doesn't care
Hitting anything
With its big orange flare

Flowing and splashing
Just like a stream
Ripping and tearing
At anything that it sees.

Samuel Newsome & Joe Land (9)
Baddow Hall Junior School

Nature Messed Up

It's so bright on Earth
The stars disappear from sight
It's so light on Earth at night
That the birds sing and fly on the wing
The flowers are blooming
When winter is looming
Oh what a wonderful messed up sight!

Sarah Austin (9)
Baddow Hall Junior School

Guy Fawkes

Fireworks, fireworks burning bright
All go up on Guy Fawkes Night
High, high up into the sky
I would like some pumpkin pie
Sparklers, rockets, Catherine wheels
I wonder how my mum's cat feels
Collecting pennies for my guy
These will buy my pumpkin pie.

Jodie Ridgewell Wright (8)
Baddow Hall Junior School

Snow Poem

I like snow
It's very cold I know
When it's cold the grass doesn't grow
When snow falls it's very slow
When it's cold the grass goes yellow
Do not slip, watch that fellow!

Hannah Gridley (9)
Baddow Hall Junior School

Rainbows

Rainbows shining all around
Over the hills and empty towns
Flowing through the empty space
Colours flowing like a race
I look up in the bright blue sky
To find a rainbow climbing high
I imagine the colours are really bright
They are like a really bright light
At the end there is a pot of gold
I'll follow it until I'm cold.

Amber Spencer (9)
Baddow Hall Junior School

The Sea

I wonder which creatures live under the sea?
I wonder what adventure awaits?
Where no light can reach
The darkness penetrates the creatures, blinding them
They cannot see, they cannot move
Without their sight they are paralysed
Their foes who are very happy to see their prey standing still!

All the creatures are unique in their own way
Which makes them special all day long
There are unusual plants along with the coral
Alive and well the sharks move in for the kill
When they return, they're hurt and sad
For not getting any lunch!

Dolphins leap high into the air
Sea horses bounce along merrily
Manta rays lay on sea floor waiting for some prey
Waves splashing on the shore
Penguins dive for squid and fish
Jellyfish moving through, stinging everything in their way
So I wish I lived in the sea with all the amazing creatures!

George Shaw (11)
Baddow Hall Junior School

My Dad

He's like a monkey
Jumping up and down
Trying to reach a banana
Without a single frown.

He scrambles through the food
Rushing around everywhere
Taking my money
Which is no way fair!

Mum nagging him every day
About him leaving hairs
They are everywhere
I wish he took more care.

Mum complaining to Dad
For not doing any work
He should be cleaning dishes
Instead of being such a jerk.

I love him to bits
Although he can be a real pain
He's still *my* dad
I love him just the same!

Lucy Peckham (10)
Baddow Hall Junior School

The Jungle

I am Tarzan, loose in the jungle
With my animal friends beside me
Ow . . . oops, I fell and hurt my knee
While I'm swinging in the coconut tree.

I am Jane lost in the jungle
Looking for my mice
I wish I had a gin and tonic
With lots of lemon and ice.

I am a tiger wandering the jungle
Looking for some food
But I'm not in a good mood
So watch out or I'll be rude.

I am a monkey in the jungle
Swinging on a vine
Looking for some bananas
To make my coat shine.

I am a lion roaring through the jungle
Looking for some prey
I'm very hungry
And I haven't had a very good day.

I am a bird flying through the jungle
Looking for some spiders to eat
Trying to keep high
So there's no hungry lions to meet.

Kelsey Fisher (10)
Baddow Hall Junior School

In The Cold

Freezing cold on a winter's day
Sitting around not knowing what to say
Asking my mum if I can go out
Then I'll shout and stamp about
When my mum changes her mind
She lets me out and I find
A snowman made out of snow
Then my mum takes me to the show.

I go and watch Goldilocks
Then I shout with all the kids
On the way home Mum buys
Some burgers, a drink and some fries
When I get home I lie on my bed
Thinking of the day ahead
My mum comes in to say goodnight
Then she turns off the light.

Hannah Newsome (8)
Baddow Hall Junior School

Snowy Day

Icy, cold, frozen snow
The birds are swooping over the lake
The birds are like wishes come true
With my big fluffy coat I feel like I'm in the love of my mother
In my warm shoes and my warm cosy scarf
I feel the love of nature right in front of me.

In the dark blue sky
The snow looks like the Northern Lights
Jack Frost makes the branches like shimmering glass
Soon I get tired and make my way in
I have big bags under my eyes
Like a heavy bag of icy snowflakes
I go upstairs and get in bed
And then I dream of the big day ahead.

Alicia Benham (8)
Baddow Hall Junior School

Space

Space is dark with lots of stars
Standing on top of Planet Mars
Looking all around for the moon
We are going to be going soon
Saying goodbye to the sun
Let's get going everyone.

Soon we will be arriving on Planet Earth,
Try not to bump and get hurt
Looking forward to seeing my mum
And Lewis, who is my chum.

Now we are home and having our tea
Dreaming of our trip with so much to see.

Nathan Brearley (8)
Baddow Hall Junior School

Summer Poem

S unshine scorching your faces
U nder the umbrellas so we don't get burnt
M y plants turning into flowers
M ummy shopping to buy ice cream
E ating lollies till I'm sick
R ide my bike till late.

Bradley Moody (10)
Darlinghurst Primary School

Winter Magic

Snow mountains with frost on the water
Ice-cold slippery frost
A polar bear roaring
The salty air
Ice-cold water.

Sarah Nash (9)
Darlinghurst Primary School

Wings
(Based on 'If I Had Wings' by Pie Corbett)

If I had wings . . .
I would touch the tallest mountain
And slip, slide back down.

If I had wings . . .
I would eat up the clouds like candyfloss
And sleep on the deep fluffiness.

If I had wings . . .
I would touch the stars
As I'm full of adrenaline.

If I had wings . . .
I would eat the moon of cheese
And sleep on the shiny surface.

If I had wings . . .
I would glide in the glistening wind
And fly all down.

Danial Nash (9)
Darlinghurst Primary School

TV

TV is good
TV is great
With really good shows
Like 'Match Of The Day'.

You can buy them
In all shapes and sizes
You can borrow some of them
Or get them as prizes.

TV is cool
Because you can watch the news
And you can see
Everyone's point of view.

Jarel Jack (9)
Darlinghurst Primary School

Wings
(Based on 'If I Had Wings' by Pie Corbett)

If I had wings . . .
I would taste the invisible air
As I glide through the blue sky.

If I had wings . . .
I would touch the white candyfloss
In the bright sky.

If I had wings . . .
I would gaze at the shimmering rivers
And streams down on Earth.

If I had wings . . .
I would hear the shiny sea
As it gleams in my eyes.

If I had wings . . .
I would smell the smoke
Coming out of the factories.

If I had wings . . .
I would dream of laying on the candyfloss
As I look down below.

Haleema Khatun (9)
Darlinghurst Primary School

Sunshine Trees

Bumpy bark under my fingers
Bitter leaves under the trees
Big bushy owls hooting at me
Shimmering sunlight over the trees
The sweet-smelling air running up to my nose.

Thomas Wright (8)
Darlinghurst Primary School

Landscape

Lovely orange and yellow mountains
Long green grass rubbing against my fingers
Smooth grey rocks falling slowly off the mountains
The calm river flowing by the grass
Fresh air going into my lungs.

Joshua Fix (8)
Darlinghurst Primary School

Wings
(Based on 'If I Had Wings' by Pie Corbett)

If I had wings . . .
I would taste the birds as if they were chicken.

If I had wings . . .
I would hear the war clashing as if it were a big cat roaring.

If I had wings . . .
I would gaze down at the shiny sea.

If I had wings . . .
I would smell the moon like cheese.

If I had wings . . .
I would dream everything was McDonald's.

If I had wings . . .
I would touch the sun.

Owen Lee Burton (8)
Darlinghurst Primary School

Wings
(Based on 'If I Had Wings' by Pie Corbett)

If I had wings . . .
I would stare at glittery stars and sit with my best mate to gaze at night.

If I had wings . . .
I would change the colour of the shiny sun and turn the world so bright.

If I had wings . . .
I would sleep on the bushy clouds and jump on the moon.

If I had wings . . .
I would listen to the birds tweeting that smile so sweetly.

If I had wings . . .
I would smell creamy ice cream going through the seaside.

If I had wings . . .
I would taste a Flake on an ice cream and dream in Heaven.

If I had wings . . .
I would dream of everyone having wings forever.

Charlotte Tanner (9)
Darlinghurst Primary School

Wings
(Based on 'If I Had Wings' by Pie Corbett)

If I had wings . . .
I would see a football match and see the winning goal.

If I had wings . . .
I would hear the roar of a crowd in the distance.

If I had wings . . .
I would touch the shiny moon and fly silently.

If I had wings . . .
I would taste the moon and it tastes like rotten cheese.

If I had wings . . .
I would smell the sweets from a sweet factory below.

If I had wings . . .
I would dream of flying forever.

Jamie Cooper (9)
Darlinghurst Primary School

Snowy Landscape

Clouds passing through me
Snowy mountains freezing my fingers
Clouds whispering around me
Fresh snowy air
Cold snow on my tongue.

Kai Davies (8)
Darlinghurst Primary School

Forest Landscape

Clouds rushing like time speeding ahead
The hard wood pressing against my hand
Trees whooshing overhead
I can smell the fresh air
I can taste the sugary leaves.

Edward Mukudu (9)
Darlinghurst Primary School

Green, Green Grass

Huge green trees and tiny bushes standing still like soldiers
The green, green grass under my hand pricking my fingers like thorns
The horrid smell of grass from yesterday's rain
The sweet air as I yawn slowly.

Lucie Wade (9)
Darlinghurst Primary School

Senses

I can see a windmill spinning around with the wind
I can smell the river rushing through
I can taste the wheat
I can hear the river
I can feel the wind.

Nathan Woollard (9)
Darlinghurst Primary School

The Shining Sun

I can see the sky shining at me
I can touch the clouds going through me
I can hear the fields rumbling
I can smell the trees and sweet branches
I can taste the clouds as they go by.

George Sadler (8)
Darlinghurst Primary School

Words

Thank you for words, if we did not have any
we would not be able to speak.
Thank you for words because we can make them sound silly
and make them sound funny.
Thank you for words that let us read.
Thank you for words that let us call each other
and thank you for words that we invented.

Max Cottage (8)
Darlinghurst Primary School

Anger, Anger

Anger is a fireball racing in the sky
Anger is a bomb hitting a car on the road
Anger is a dragon breathing fire and smoke
Anger is a building blowing up into pieces
Anger is a volcano squirting out lava
Anger is lightning crashing together
Anger is thunder crashing together
Anger is waves hitting the sea
Anger is a boat hitting the rock
Anger is red fire
Anger is bad.

Olivia Inskip-Hickey (9)
Fairways Primary School

Summer's Sight

Galloped through the field did she
Gentle as the lapping sea
Running like lightning fire
Yet her beauty will never tire
Mane and tail whipped in wind
As the light slowly dimmed
On her flanks moonlight shone
My horrid thoughts have now gone.

Oh damn that fence that holds her in
For she is such a beautiful thing
Ah my friend and oh my foes
Watch her trot upon her toes
Her haunting eyes
Her whining cries
Now I must say my goodbyes.

Lauren Jefferies (10)
Fairways Primary School

Witch's Spell

Rat's tail, bat's wing, eye of toad, in they pile, round they go
Stringy guts of a whale, in goes the yellow toenail
Rat's tail, bat's wing, eye of toad, in they pile, round they go
Tail of monkey, foot of cat, throw in an extra gut of a bat
Rat's tail, bat's wing, eye of toad, in they pile, round they go
Plenty of bloodshot eyes and a few gruesome flies
Rat's tail, bat's wing, eye of toad, in they pile, round they go.

Amanda Bowers (10)
Fairways Primary School

Witch's Spell

Cauldron bubble, cauldron bubble
Getting ready for lots of trouble
Stripe of zebra, sewer rat
Mouldy toenails double, double.

Old men's slippers hop into the pot
Small baby fallen from cot
Sandy foot, wax from ear
Slithering snake, have no fear.

Cauldron bubble, cauldron bubble
Nearly ready for lots of trouble
Stripe of zebra, sewer rat
Mouldy toenails double, double.

Llama's spit from mouth fresh
Stale milk and blind bat's flesh
Spider's web, great whale's eye
All pig's lungs from one big sty.

Cauldron bubble, cauldron bubble
Now we're ready for lots of trouble
Stripe of zebra, sewer rat
Mouldy toenails double, double.

Anna Lawrance (10)
Fairways Primary School

Emotional Poem

As I walked round the yard
It seemed frightfully hard
To remember the day
When my cat passed away
His picture on the wall
As I started to bawl.

His gentle soft purring
Like a quiet whirring
A hole in my bruised heart
As we both have to part
My heart will never ever mend
As I say goodbye to my dearest friend.

Bethany Kiamil (11)
Fairways Primary School

A Romantic Poem

In a field oh so far away
I happily knew something of great wealth
It would impact me every day
No one beside me except myself.

By me an oak tree stood beside
A grasshopper chirped contentedly
The long grass swaying like the tide
Feeling oh so solitary.

For over cottage and palisade
Over lake and dirty pigsty
Over green field and dancing glade
For very, very lonely over these was I.

I look and see swaying grass
Nothing for miles and miles around
No humble cottage, no shard of glass
Good to be alone, so profound.

I think back on this every day
It made me feel unbelievable
It made me happy in every way
I had not a care at all.

I think when I lay in my bed
I'm in shallow or pensive thought
I have that image in my head
In pouring rain or bone-dry drought.

Daniel Lewis (11)
Fairways Primary School

Love

Shall I compare thee to a bright spring day
Where everything comes to life in April and in May?
Like tweeting birds flying around
To me you cost more than one hundred pounds
Your brown glossy hair shimmers in the sun
You will always be my one chum
You are my sunshine, you are my rain
For we will go on together like a daisy chain.

Rachel Morris (10)
Fairways Primary School

Fear

Fear tastes like pure coal
Fear feels like an ice-cold shudder running down your spine
Fear looks like a shadow following you for all eternity
Fear is silent and swift
Fear sounds like a scream of horror crying for help.

Owain Tomlin (10)
Fairways Primary School

Happiness Is . . .

Happiness is . . .
Getting £1,000 for free
When you get a house
Eating sweets all day
Getting all the PS2 games
Buying a fifty-inch flat screen TV
Someone being your slave
A robot cooking for you.

Iwan Tomlin (8)
Fairways Primary School

Happiness Is . . .

Happiness is . . .
My sister laughing
The colours of orange and yellow
Playing with my best friend Bethany
Getting a certificate
Watching my fish swim around
Getting a token
Eating chocolate with my sister
Reading with Bethany T my best friend
Miss Bradley-Mason and Mr Joyce teaching us.

Jessica Bunting (8)
Fairways Primary School

Happiness Is . . .

Happiness is . . .
Making a sandcastle
Eating a chocolate bar
Playing with your friends
Having a house all to yourself
Playing with your friend at home.

Hollie Zucker (7)
Fairways Primary School

Happiness Is . . .

Happiness is . . .
When you make a new friend
Have a whole jar of chocolate spread
Making someone's day
Giving a present to someone
Getting a kiss from my boyfriend.

Kate Ridley (7)
Fairways Primary School

Zechariah

Zechariah was in the temple
Praying for all the people
When an angel came to say
Elizabeth would have a baby boy
All the people would come and say hip hip hooray
They would look at him and go and pray
He would be a special boy
Cherished with loads of joy
He went back home with no voice
He did not have a choice.

Zoe Bolton-Smith (11)
Fairways Primary School

Jesus

The Son of God
The baby of Mary
Was born in a stable
With love from everyone.

He is the man
Who healed us all
And was given the gifts
Myrrh, frankincense and gold.

The Son of God
The baby of Mary
Was born in a stable
With love from everyone.

Angel Gabriel came down to Earth
Exclaimed to Mary, 'Be calm,
Don't be frightened, you will have a baby,
The Son of God, you will call him Jesus.'

The Son of God
The baby of Mary
Was born in a stable
With love from everyone.

Léoni Hughes (10)
Fairways Primary School

The Sun

The sun is a cloud of fire
The sun is pure as gold
The sun is as bright as the moon
The sun is the best of all
The sun's flames are as bright as light
The sun is the best of all.

Tara Said (9)
Fairways Primary School

Anger Is . . .

Anger is . . .
Clouds crashing
Thunder and lightning banging
My teacher shouting
Children shouting in the playground
Two fireworks going off
A volcano exploding.

Chloe Denby (8)
Fairways Primary School

Anger!

Anger is a boat splashing on the rocks
Anger is a girl breaking a glass
Anger is like a burning fireball
Anger is like lightning crashing
Anger is like a volcano exploding
Anger is like fire
Anger is like a dragon breathing fire
Anger is like an oven burning.

Jade Shaw (9)
Fairways Primary School

Happiness Is . . .

Happiness is kissing my boyfriend
Happiness is kissing my mum goodnight
Happiness is the sun shining
It is like a rose shining in the sun
Happiness is the river sparkling everywhere
It's like children laughing
Happiness is singing.

Jessica-May Davey (8)
Fairways Primary School

Winter's Spell

Snow, snow
Feathery snowflakes in the breeze
Now the bright red stockings are hung up
On the gleaming Christmas tree
Winter, winter
The shimmering moon
Beautiful lumps of snow are piling up
Elves are dancing and prancing about
Lovely, lovely snow
Snow, snow
Feathery snowflakes in the breeze!

Megan Preece (9)
Fairways Primary School

Anger

Anger is like an oven burning
Anger is like a red blazing fireball
Anger is like a burning iron
Anger is like touching the bright yellow sun
Anger is like glaring red and orange
Anger makes you scream and snap
Anger makes you shout and bellow.

Georgia Stoneham (9)
Fairways Primary School

The Magic Box
(Based on 'Magic Box' by Kit Wright)

I will put in my box . . .
Sparks of electricity to brighten homes
The warmth of the great big sun
Water from the clear blue sea.

I will put in my box . . .
Hope for everyone
Clattering money for those in need
The puffy white clouds.

I will put in my box . . .
The wind for people to breathe
A hospital for people with illnesses
Parents for every child.

My box is made from care and love
Diamonds and crystals and most of all hope.

Becky Thwaites (10)
Great Waltham CE Primary School

Magic Box
(Based on 'Magic Box' by Kit Wright)

In the box I'd put . . .
The texture of sticky chewy toffee
The smell of apple pie
And the taste of sausages.

In the box I'd put . . .
The warmth of the dragon's stomach
To take away the coldness of the ice man's breath
And a pet for every person to keep them company.

In the box I'd put . . .
The biggest ever rainbow
Every star and the cherry trees
I'd go around the village
Giving things to the rich and poor.

It's decorated with hinges of gold
A dragon on the lid
That's my box.

Reece Field (10)
Great Waltham CE Primary School

Magic Box
(Based on 'Magic Box' by Kit Wright)

I will put in my box . . .
The natural world from prehistoric life
The warmth for all trees with fur and animals with leaves.

I will put in my box . . .
The tooth from a T-rex
And the head from the Queen, edible clothes for all.

I will put in my box . . .
Schools with great education
And chocolates for myself and food just for me.

I will put in my box . . .
Lots of forgiveness and the beauty of everyone
And last of all the beautiful sunset.

Robert Green (10)
Great Waltham CE Primary School

Magic Box
(Based on 'Magi Box' by Kit Wright)

I will put in my box . . .
The smell of fresh bread
The cool wet rain
The heat from a fire so that the poor stay warm.

I will put in my box . . .
Food for poor people who can't afford food.

I will put in the box . . .
Fresh water for those who don't have any
And will starve if they don't get it.

I will put in my box . . .
A newborn baby to give to someone who cares.

I will put in my box . . .
A good dream for someone to dream.

I will put in my box . . .
A secret, a big secret.

I will put in my box . . .
Warmth and happiness for the world.

Bethan Culling (11)
Great Waltham CE Primary School

My Magic Box
(Based on 'Magic Box' by Kit Wright)

In my box . . .
Families to be safe and healthy.

In my box . . .
A big fat turkey for Christmas dinner.

In my box . . .
Fresh water for the thirsty.

In my box . . .
I would like toothbrushes and toothpaste for everyone.

In my box . . .
I would like new houses for the poor.

In my box . . .
I would like clean clothes.

In my box . . .
I would like to have a football for entertainment.

In my box . . .
I would love a mum or a dad to hug a poor child.

Cameron Worcester (10)
Great Waltham CE Primary School

Magic Box Poem

(Based on 'Magic Box' by Kit Wright)

I will put in my box . . .
The many shades of the sunset
So very beautiful but not always useful.

I will put in my box . . ,
Water for the whole village
To stop drought dampening hearts
And food for the poor to stop hunger.

I will put in my box . . .
The rich velvety robes for wealth
Rags for those less fortunate
But for once swap them around.

I will put in my box . . .
The chuckle of a proud father
The smile of a kind mother
The dreams and wishes of a child.

My box is covered with hopes of a better future
With silver and gold in the corners.

It whizzes round the village spreading happiness to all
To men and women, boys and girls
Rich and poor, young and old.

Catherine Warner (11)
Great Waltham CE Primary School

My Magic Box
(Based on 'Magic Box' by Kit Wright)

In my magic box I would put . . .
The cool breeze of the market when the wind is brushing through
 your hair
The hot sun bringing warmth to the heart of others
The refreshing rain after a long hot summer.

In my box I would put . . .
The sound of a cockerel waking the villages
The song of the bluebirds singing peace to all
The laughter of children playing outside
The rustling leaves floating to the ground.

In my box I would put . . .
The smell of freshly baked bread
You reach out to take the bread but someone rushes past taking it first
The soft texture of the warm doughy bread is all that you have left to
 dream about.

I would put in my box . . .
The colour a baby gives when it opens up its eyes and smiles at you
 for the first time
The rosy cheeks of a child on a winter's day.

In my box I would put . . .
The taste of hot chocolate
An apple freshly picked from a tree
Corn harvested from your own field.

My box is decorated with satin, gold stars and beautiful sequins
That represent the lives of those that have passed away
The lock on my box is a lock of hope, secrets and *love*.

I will set my box free on a journey of discovery
Across the sea to the global village and it will bring peace to all.

Josie Coventry (11)
Great Waltham CE Primary School

Magic Box
(Based on 'Magic Box' by Kit Wright)

I will put in my box . . .
The sight of a sunny day and water falling on trees and rocks
The smell of freshly baked bread and roast chicken.

I will put in my box . . .
The sound of the birds and the swishing wind
A smooth quilt to cover people when the night is cold.

I will put in my box . . .
Colours red, yellow, orange and green
With the cool breeze.

I will fashion my box with gold and silver sequins
And natural things, that's what I will put in my box.

Jenny Armstrong (10)
Great Waltham CE Primary School

The Magic Box
(Based on 'Magic Box' by Kit Wright)

In my box I would put . . .
The last dream of a comedian
Dreams of fun and games
And the hope of a child.

In my box I would put . . .
A game of chequers or chess
The pleasure of winning
And the forgiveness of losing.

My box would be fashioned from basic and fun material
And the hinges would be tiddly winks
My box would be given to the poor to help.

Daniel Andrews (11)
Great Waltham CE Primary School

I Would Put In The Box . . .
(Based on 'Magic Box' by Kit Wright)

I would put in my box . . .
A bouncing beautiful bunny and some clucking chickens
Some clean water, a yellow moon and a white sun.

I would put in my box . . .
Lots of lovely lakes
Grinning, groaning goats in the farm
Big bears building houses.

I would put in my box . .
A fiery red dragon with flames as hot as sparks
A polar bear as cold as ice
A big elephant and a tiny mouse.

I would put in my box . . .
Boiling ice cream and freezing apple crumble
A cheetah as slow as a snail
And a snail as fast as a cheetah.

I would put in my box . . .
A lot of rain pitter-pattering on the window in the summer
Sunny blistering days in the winter.

Matty Read & Joshua De'ath (10)
Great Waltham CE Primary School

Magic Box
(Based on 'Magic Box' by Kit Wright)

I will put in my box . . .
A waving river for those who have to walk miles for a little to drink.

I will put in the box . . .
The leaves falling in winter and the snow skating in autumn.

I will put in the box . . .
A thirteenth planet and the miaowing of a dog
And the barking of a cat.

I will put in my box . . .
A new world with new kind people as a new baby awakens.

I will put in my box . . .
A world for unhappy people and send all the unhappy people there.

I will put in my box . . .
Happy dreams for sad children to brighten up their lives.

I will put in my box . . .
A happy world with happy people for a happy life.

Elsie Hayes (9)
Great Waltham CE Primary School

My Magic Box
(Based on 'Magic Box' by Kit Wright)

I will put into the box . . .
A massive city with skyscrapers, strong and tall
A tiny town with mud flats, small and weak.

I will put into the box . . .
The crunching sounds of feet on a desert dry
And the rushing river hitting rocks.

I will put into the box . . .
Fresh fruit and a little money for the poor
A vacuum to take a little money from the rich to share it all out.

I will put into the box . . .
Flames of the sun to warm the poor
And icebergs to cool down the wealthy.

I will decorate my box with sand from the hottest desert
And the blue of the bluest sea
The greens of the greenest grass
The whitest white of a star.

Thomas Strangwige (10)
Great Waltham CE Primary School

The Magic Box
(Based on 'Magic Box' by Kit Wright)

I will put in my box . . .
The world's largest chess and draughts board ready for use
And the walls of skeletons guarding this beauty
Only the wisest will open the box.

I will put in my box . . .
The great gold that perches on the walls and roof
But if the box is opened forcibly it will turn red.

I will put in my box . . .
The heat of the world controlled by a dragon
Heating the entire village.

I will put in my box . . .
The power of electricity controlled by lightning
With a kite with a key stuck in a tree which controls the lightning.

I will put in my box . . .
The clouds with fresh water, crystal clear and clean
Perfect for drinking and good for cleaning
What a box!

Samuel Tyler (10)
Great Waltham CE Primary School

My Magic Box
(Based on 'Magic Box' by Kit Wright)

I will put in my box . . .
The smell of freshly baked apple pie
And the taste of freshly baked bread
And roast chicken with crispy potatoes.

I will put in my box . . .
The sound of a whistling bird
The sound of a trickling stream
And the sound of a school bell ringing.

I will put in my box . . .
A laugh of a baby
The baby's first steps
And a baby's first word.

The box will have ice hinges
The lock will be made from crocodile's teeth
And the corners made from gold.

Victoria Hawes (11)
Great Waltham CE Primary School

The Village Changer
(Based on 'Magic Box' by Kit Wright)

I will put in my box . . .
Burgers and fast food
A high definition TV
And a city of blinding lights.

I will put in my box . . .
Clean water as soft as silk
Chocolate bars and sweets
Sausages cooked on a barbecue.

I will put in my box . . .
A smell of apple pie
The hunt for freshly ground coffee
A smell of bacon.

My box is made with sequins and stars
With secrets everywhere
I will send my box to the global village
And let it open for those in need.

George Martin (9)
Great Waltham CE Primary School

The Magic Box
(Based on 'Magic Box' by Kit Wright)

I will put in my box . . .
A flowing waterfall that shines in the light
The sound of a hissing snake
The smell of a hot curry.

I will put in my box . . .
A bright flower for sad people
And a beach full of happy people
A sun in winter and snow in summer.

I will put in my box . . .
Children playing in the park
Having a great time
And secrets right at the bottom.

I will put in my box . . .
Stars floating in the air
Beds for people sitting on the streets
And PlayStations for a bit of fun.

Victoria Seymour (11)
Great Waltham CE Primary School

The Box
(Based on 'Magic Box' by Kit Wright)

I will put in the box . . .
A tamed dragon with a fiery tale that will do no harm.

I will put in the box . . .
The hopes and dreams of a child and mother
A cow for a farm and puppies for kids.

I will put in the box . . .
Happiness for everybody, but especially the needy.

My box is fashioned from iron, steel, gold and fire!

George Dodd (9)
Great Waltham CE Primary School

My Magic Box
(Based on 'Magic Box' by Kit Wright)

I will put in my box . . .
A blazing hot ball of gas known as the sun
The moon and stars as they shine as dawn is nigh.

I will put in my box . . .
The smell of warm tomato soup on a cold day
Fresh crusty bread with butter.

I will put in my box . .
A baby as it awakens from a heavy sleep
The whistle of a kind pet owner calling his dog
A lovely feast for the whole village to enjoy
The most rare animal in the universe
Maybe even a new unknown species.

I will fashion my box with the first flower of spring
And the last leaf in winter to fall off a tree.

I will put in my box . . .
The highest peak of Mount Everest
And the deepest, darkest gush of water
From the deepest, biggest lake that you have ever seen.

I will put in my box . . .
An elephant's squeak and a mouse's bellow.

I hope that my box will take all pathways to a better future
With more hope, imagination and affection for each other
I will put in my box everything special!

Morgan Gentry (10)
Great Waltham CE Primary School

Starvation

He creeps into every nook and cranny like a devious monster.
He is like maggots eating away in your stomach.
He sucks your life out until you are skin and bones.
Starvation is an enemy to love and kindness.
He crunches the bones of young children
As he hears the screaming of stomachs
As he leaves them cold and lifeless!

Holly Hawkins (11)
St John's CE Primary School, Danbury

Starvation

It's like a world without sunshine,
A bird called Starvation blocking our freedom.
He swoops here and there.
Starvation is a prison of darkness,
A weapon against us.
No energy, empty stomachs,
Crying, screaming.
He dominates and holds people at his mercy.
The power makes him laugh gleefully.
Starvation is a growing headache.
Hungriness causes a smack as it hits the vulnerable.
The weakness causes the death and emptiness.

Stephanie Ovenden (10)
St John's CE Primary School, Danbury

Starvation

The starvation period takes over the soul.
And sucks it out, merciless, cruel and monstrous,
Destroying the lives of African people.
Only a tiny portion of food for a week,
The hunger and the suffering brings misery to others,
People help each other and work as a team
To stick together, giving hope for the future.

Conner Austin (10)
St John's CE Primary School, Danbury

Starvation

Starvation creeps upon you like a cold winter's day,
Starvation eats out your appetite,
Starvation is like being drawn into a river without a breath,
Starvation is like an ogre
Stopping you crossing the bridge to a land full of food.

Lewis Simmons (10)
St John's CE Primary School, Danbury

Starvation

The reporters asked the question, 'Are you hungry?'
Scream, groan, the people cry,
Yet none come to help, only question.
Starvation is crawling inside
Then haunting them like a bad dream,
It is worse than any bruise or broken bone,
It is certain death.

The Devil laughs as weeping is all over countries;
No hope, no hand of aid - such a cruel world.

Mark Bandell (11)
St John's CE Primary School, Danbury

Starvation

He slowly crawls among others,
Empty and dying of hunger and thirst,
A shadow creeping up on you,
A great beast.
There is weakness in your body,
There is screaming,
There is silence,
It is a nightmare - starvation.

Joshua Warner (11)
St John's CE Primary School, Danbury

The Sea

The sea is a hungry dog
The sea is mean and angry
The sea is rough and bloodthirsty
The sea crashes on the rocks
The sea thunders on the cliffs
Roars like a fierce lion
Raging bull charging savagely
Mad like a monkey
Once the storm has gone
The sea is gentle and kind
Smooth but calm
Laps and glides
Glides along the seafront
And strokes the sand
Ripples on top of the sea,
The sea is calm once again.

Stuart Allen (10)
St John's CE Primary School, Danbury

The Sea

The angry waves crash violently on the shore
The sea roars angrily at the beach
The waves smashing against the cliffs
The smooth sea is more gentle now
The loving sea moves softly and slowly.

Megan Obeney (9)
St John's CE Primary School, Danbury

The Sea

The waves of the sea bash people
Over like a violent bull trying to catch its prey.

The gentle sea tickling our feet making us laugh loudly
Smoothly it breathes in and out like a white horse does.

The angry sea hitting me as I swim enjoying my day
As I play people bathing trying to get a tan.

The gliding sea, roars at the cliffs trying to make them fall
The roars are loud scaring people away.

Samuel Rye (10)
St John's CE Primary School, Danbury

The Sea

The angry waves crash violently on the shore.
The vicious waves bite at the rocks like an angry dog.
The river-blue waves smash against each other.
Then the sun comes out, the sea starts swelling, it ripples lovingly.
The tide fades into the distance, the rocks come back.
The crabs start running, fishes start swimming for their lives.

Max Harding (9)
St John's CE Primary School, Danbury

The Sea

The sea is like a ball rushing into the solid cliff
It smashes and crashes and bashes so amazingly loud
The sea is like a wild white horse running away
Cliffs are torn apart by the roaring sea
Waves thunder around away from the sand
It seems like there is a lion eating at the cliffs
It fiercely sways all over the place
The sea is an angry cheetah chasing its prey.

The storm has come to a halt.
It strokes the soft sand,
It likes to ripple, slowly in a relaxing way.
It is so peaceful and gentle the blues, greens and purples, so calming.
The breeze slowly blows at the smooth sea.
It lovingly brushes the soft beige sand.
The sun is beaming onto the calm waters.
Everyone paddles in the soft, smooth, calm shadows.
It is breathing in and out so slowly
It is like you could stay all day.

Hannah Norris (10)
St John's CE Primary School, Danbury

The Sea

The sea is a violent horse charging up the beach,
Waves crash against the rocks viciously - like a bull throwing
itself at them.
The see is rolling over, fiercely smashing against the coast,
Waves are foaming, violently crashing on the rocks.
The waves are white horses, their hooves pounding, racing
up the beach.
The angry waves are tumbling and twirling, gnawing away the shore
Twisting and turning, tumbling and rolling against the beach,
Maybe it's coming for me!
Now the sea is calming down, stroking the pebbles lovingly,
Gently the sea ripples along in a canyon,
The sun glistens on the turquoise sheet sparkling peacefully,
The sea breaks in and out on the golden sand softly.
The sea flows along smoothly in a sleek way,
Little waves splash against the rocks giving them a drink.
The day is ending now.

Sophie Huntley (10)
St John's CE Primary School, Danbury

The Sea

The sea is a vicious sea dog biting at the pebbly seashore!
Thundering white horses gallop rapidly back and forth.
The sea is like an emerald-green tiger smashing nearby rocks!
The sea roars angrily when it makes rocks cascade down off the cliffs.
The sea is dying down to a soft ripple in the breeze.
The blues and greens flow softly and splash against the rocks.
The soft sea bobs up and down in the lovely breeze.
The sun's rays gently stroke the calm sea.

Michael Boyd (9)
St John's CE Primary School, Danbury

The Sea

The sea is a murderous burglar, stealing the rocks from the cliff
The rocks are like stone giants, never to move again.
The waves crash against the rocks like a lion ready for dinner,
Rumbling crashes like a bull charging on the sand.
The bloodthirsty sea takes people out with its roaring waves.
The sea gets calmer and grinds to a halt,
The sea laps over the sand like a human stroking the sea,
The colour is sapphire-blue and a little emerald-green.
It's lovely and smooth on the surface.
The sea is bubbling very gently around the rocks.
People are sunbathing while the sea tickles their toes.
The sea flows with the current, the day is over and the people have gone.

Joshua Crowe (8)
St John's CE Primary School, Danbury

The Sea

The angry sea violently on the shore
The cruel sea crashes at the rocks
The vicious sea angrily smashes everything in its path, then
The calm sea is like a butterfly that spreads its wings and flies away.

Andrew Smiley (8)
St John's CE Primary School, Danbury

The Sea

The sea is a wild animal,
That plucks off parts of cliffs.
The sea cascades at the rocks like a charging bull.
As it roars angrily at them.
The sea is an angry person.
That crashes against the cliffs,
Waves bash against the cliffs,
Throwing white froth at them.
Waves roar angrily like a wild animal
As they crash against the rocks.

The calm sea strokes the sand
Like a hairbrush on your hair,
The peaceful blue sea is a human being, breathing in and out.
The blue, turquoise and green sea is a smooth piece of paper,
The sea ripples calmly onto the sand,
As they calmly ripple up.
The sea glides to the rocks
And to the sand,
White froth coming up to the rock
And people swim in the calm blue sea.

Amelia Western (9)
St John's CE Primary School, Danbury

The Sea

The sea is a very angry horse, galloping, hungry and wants his tea.
He gets his family and friends to join him.
They all tumble and crash until they get to the beach.
They then see nobody around and say a mean word,
And cascade back into the sea.
They are mad, they are cruel, they are vicious overall.
They want their juicy dinner.
They see the sun coming out and hide, ready to join the murderous weather again.
Quieter, quieter, quieter, the sea calms down and all you can see is the splashing of the waves.
It strokes the pebbles gently and the people come back to the beach.
They laugh and they play when it is a lovely day.
The sea smoothly flows onto their feet, the sea looks like a sheet of sapphires sparkling, twinkling in the sun.
The people splash into the sea, which bubbles gently and all the fish come out to play.
Suddenly it all falls dark and the people go away.

Rebecca Manning (10)
St John's CE Primary School, Danbury

The Sea

The angry waves crash violently on the shore.
The waves are like an angry dog eating the rocks.
The sea drags away the shells and pebbles.
A lovely calm day with the people swimming in the sea and they are sunbathing.
Loads of yachts sailing as well.
The rough waves have gone and it is a smooth sea day.

Sean Madle (9)
St John's CE Primary School, Danbury

The Sea!

The sea is a vigorous vulture searching bloodthirstily for rotting meat, causing avalanches in the ragged rocks slowly being smashed away. The jagged rocks slowly going away and the vulture can find meat, when it's had its fill it will go away.
Storm is great and the vulture eats all your dead meat and you!
But when the sea is calm it's a little fish nibbling away at the algae on the rocks and he will be back another day.
Slowly . . . slowly . . . nibbling away, the rocks slowly going, not to be back another day when the little fish finishes quite a bit.
An avalanche may take place to cause a tidal wave but do not be afraid, this takes a very long time because the little fish does it in little bites.
But if it does happen be very afraid because the extremely calm sea will turn into *an extremely rough sea!*

Thomas Braben (10)
St John's CE Primary School, Danbury

The Sea

The sea is a roaring lion, crashing viciously towards the shore,
like galloping white horses, and a violent wave tumbles all day,
back and forth relentlessly non-stop.
Then, as the day goes by, the sun slowly strokes the tips of the water.
as it tickles the pebbles and the sky turns red and reflects on the sea.

Andrew Hariz (9)
St John's CE Primary School, Danbury

The Sea

The angry sea crashes violently on the shore.
The cruel sea smashes wildly at the poor rocks
The violent sea viciously demolishes everything in its way.
The wind roars at the raging sea.
Then there's the calm sea that sways gently through the rocks.
The smooth sea is like a butterfly that spreads its wings and lovingly flies, brushing and healing.
The sea laps and nestles in the pebbles and moves softly through the sand bed.
Finds treasure as it heads towards the world of water.

Fern Gossett (10)
St John's CE Primary School, Danbury

The Sea

The sea is a raging bull charging at the rocks
The sea is a vicious dog smashing against the rock
The raging sea is like a cascade across the beach
The pounding white horses are foaming up the beach
The vicious sea plucks out the rocks
As the calm sea ripples like a calm silver stream
As the turquoise blue sea breathes in and out on the shore
As the children splash in the summer sea
The sea ripples on the shore and as we paddle in the summer sun
The storm has gone so we are having fun playing in the sea
The long summer sun and the sea laps on the sand
The peaceful sea strokes the sand smoothly
As the gentle sea brushes off the soft sand
The sea swells gently on the peaceful sand on the shore
The sea smoothly ripples on top of the smooth sand.

Heather Dorrell (9)
St John's CE Primary School, Danbury

The Sea

Wavy and has fish, seagulls and prowling sharks, sea horses
                                                                       and dolphins.
The sea is calm and blue
It is something peaceful and something angry and rough.
The sea swoops the rocks into the sea and the fish come up from the sea all brave and then the fish come up and the sharks eat the fish.

Joe O'Sullivan (9)
St John's CE Primary School, Danbury

The Sea

The sea goes *swish, swish* on a hard, wet day
Nothing to do at the beach than play, play, play
The sea is a smashing otter, a rolling scary creature
It roars just like a tiger, it bangs like it's been shot
It's raging like it's coming to get us, tumbling down the rough rock
The sun has come out, the sea is a calm animal
It's been smooth like it's been flattened, it's bubbling like a hot bath
It's swelling nice and gently, it's loving and it's calming
The sea is a best friend to me.

Adam Knights (9)
St John's CE Primary School, Danbury

The Sea

The sea is like a raging bear trying to get food,
The waves are like violent dogs barking and smashing at the door,
The sea is like a fierce wolf jumping and crawling everywhere.
Cliffs are flaking because of the sea.
The waves are as mad as the sea, they're bashing everything,
The sand disappears because they have got it all,
And are not letting it out.
Cliffs are like mad sharks trying to stay up. Waves are like big rollers,
Rolling on the rocks.
The sea is a person breathing in and out.
The cliffs are losing shape because of the violent waves.
The sea is like a soft dog now the storm is going.
The waves have calmed down now they have actually disappeared.
The sea is like a smooth pond.

Chantelle Haley (9)
St John's CE Primary School, Danbury

The Sea

The raging sea is starved and thirsty, smashing everything in its way!
Pushing, pulling, biting off chunks of stone off the cliff.
Herds of white horses careering at the beach, violently hitting the
ground, then being pulled back in as the next row hits the shore.
The sound of the wind screaming over the water, water taunting
                                                        the waves.
The dark sky blackens the sea to a craggy piece of slate.

The sun's blinding beams stretch across the water turning it to a
sapphire-blue, gently lapping at the shore, pulling in some grains
                                                        of sand.
Little ripples crossing the water slowly stroking the sand over and over
Pieces of driftwood floating over the water being driven by the
                                                    little splashes.

Felix Flechtner (10)
St John's CE Primary School, Danbury

Starvation

Starvation is cruel
It is like someone taking food out of you
Starvation is making people beg for food
People are empty just because of starvation
People are really hungry, desperate for something to eat
When you are round people in starvation you hear choking
                                            and coughing

Along with the crying
They are dying.

Rebecca Perkins (10)
St John's CE Primary School, Danbury

The Sea

The sea is like exploding fireworks,
The sea is exploding fireworks,
As gentle as a sheet of paper,
As smooth as a new piece of wood,
Banging like the mansion destroyed,
Smashing like the rocks falling,
Crashing like the biggest car crash ever,
As calm as the quietest music ever,
As soft as the TV screen.

Nicholas Perkins (9)
St John's CE Primary School, Danbury

Snowballs

When I looked out of my window
I was filled with delight,
It was something cold and white.
I got my gloves on and my hat,
And went out the doors, just like that!
I found my friends and got some snow,
To throw at my most hated foe.
We dodged and ducked and threw and we chucked,
And then we went in,
With a bright red chin
And finally had some cocoa.

Edward Dowling (9)
The Daiglen School

Red

Red is the sunset when it is getting dark,
It is my fish swimming by in its tank,
It makes me feel fast and excited,
It makes me feel like Speedy Gonzalez.

Red is for Arsenal, the champions of the world,
It is also for anger, for shouting and screaming,
It is for apples that are healthy,
And for blood that makes you scared.

Samuel Apata (9)
The Daiglen School

Red

Red makes me feel hot with fire,
It is blood falling in a battlefield,
It makes me feel good and bold.

Red makes me go blushy,
It reminds me of embarrassing moments,
Red makes me scared and I curl up in bed.

Red is fast, like winning a race,
It is the very colour of
Fish swimming in the sea.

Red is my favourite colour,
It is fun and it is sad,
That's why I like red.

Joseph Klein (8)
The Daiglen School

Brown

Brown is nature all around
Hot chocolate for you and me
The monkeys on the trees
My chair that I'm sitting on right now.

Brown makes me feel hot inside,
It makes me think of an away match
It reminds me of my hair
Now I want chocolate!

Harry Osborn (8)
The Daiglen School

Brown

Brown is the colour that makes me shine
It is chocolate for me,
It is the soft earth,
It is a bear.

Brown is wooden furniture,
It is houses.
It is like a star in the sky,
It is mud here on the ground.

Jack Jenkins (9)
The Daiglen School

The Ancient Ice Planet

In the cold land where glittery caves are.
Where the frozen rivers and ponds stay.
The icy mountains and the warm domes are cosy.
The glaciers are like white icing and no rock can be seen.
There is no living thing and it is extremely peaceful.
Nearly everything is ice and snow.

Max Rabey (8)
The Daiglen School

Red

Red is the sign of anger slithering through you,
The anger makes you strong.
Blood dripping from a broken nose,
A big round face filled with anger.

Red is the blood in people's mouths after a war,
In war there must be anger.
The Devil is as hot as fire,
Running as fast as lightning with a dagger in your hand.

Red is the strength in your hands,
The brain with blood pumping,
The Great Fire of London,
Your ears are red when you're shy.

Peter Piskov (8)
The Daiglen School

One To Ten

One white wallaby was wearing a wicked waistcoat.
Two tiny tigers trotted towards a tree.
Three thin thermometers threw a thistle.
Four forgotten forests followed a foreigner.
Five fishermen were filthy.
Six sick signals were silent.
Seven seedlings were separated from September.
Eight enthusiastic people were using equipment.
Nine nibbling nephews were nicking a neighbour.
Ten tennis players had a tender tentacle.

Nana Kwasi Dartey-Baah Jnr (8)
The Daiglen School

One To Ten

One white wallaby was wearing wacky wellies.
Two terrific teapots took tea together.
Three thin thumbs thought things
Four funny foals from France
Five fat flies flying fast
Six squashed snakes sitting in the sun
Seven scary spiders sitting scaring
Eight angry anacondas ate apples.
Nine naughty notes nibbling nuts
Ten tortoises talking thoughtfully.

Eddie Williams (7)
The Daiglen School

One To Ten

One white wallaby was wearing wacky wellies.
Two tiny teenagers were tied up to a tiger.
Three thin thesauruses were playing in the theme park.
Four forests were flipping for fun.
Five fizzy drinks were feeling foolish because they fainted.
Six sick signs were silly.
Seven snails were silent for sixty seconds.
Eight elephants were eating with eighty other elephants.
Nine naked nails were nibbling on nuts.
Ten T-rexes were terrorising toys.

Zachary Cannon (7)
The Daiglen School

Déjà Vu

Once there was a boy who
Was taken around his new house,
The lady who showed him round
Wore the same blunt but sweet perfume his mother wore.
He walked down the corridors feeling the walls.
As if he had been there before.

Miles Barella (10)
The Daiglen School

My Hamster Cookie

My dear old Cookie,
You're up in Heaven;
Why didn't you live till you were seven?
You were three years old
And your fur looked like gold.

Louis Hart (10)
The Daiglen School

Safe Homes

H omes, homes
O h I hope I get one
M any people have them
E ven though some people don't
S helter is a need for everyone.

Alex Minkey (9)
The Daiglen School

West Ham United

Every time I see West Ham United
I always feel so delighted
To see them score home and away
Really makes the greatest day
Bobby Moore was the best
When he wore the claret and blue crest
The English nation cried and cried
On the sad day that he died
But I'll remember him forever on
As long as I sing the West Ham song
West Ham is my favourite team
Supporting them is like a dream.

Jack Sansom (9)
The Daiglen School

The Poppy

The poppy is a flower.
It rises from the ground
The poppy rises through the depths of battle
People will say it's their finest hour

In the war the poppy was a sign
For peace and a new start.
So let the war be over
And peace for everyone!

George Jamieson (9)
The Daiglen School

David Beckham

He is a tough piece of meat with his strength,
The leader of the team,
He is also white with the colour of his shirt,
A hawk as fast as lightning,
A bird flying free around the pitch.

Joshua Butt (10)
The Daiglen School

Jesse McCartney

A man that sings like a lark.
Good thing he does not bark,
Quick like a swordfish,
Slick like a puma.
What a man, really grand.
Having fun in the sun.
He goes to girls,
Ends up being kissed but if
He changes his attitude he will
Be missed.
He's a show-off parrot
Like a dove.
Over all he is a great singer.

Onur Sevigen (10)
The Daiglen School

One To Ten

One white wallaby was walking with a wagon.
Two tiny teenagers had a tug of war.
Three thoughtful thesauruses thought things.
Four frightened freckled fish went away for a fortnight.
Five floppy frogs were flung and landed flat in the road.
Six slimy slugs went on their scooters and saw a sculpture of seaweed.
Seven spiky spirits split sprouts.
Eight enemies escaped Egypt.
Nine nosy nails nodded.
Ten tricky troops fell in a tub.

Lewis Woollard (7)
The Daiglen School

Mirror

'Mirror, Mirror on the wall,
Will I stay small or grow tall?'
'Fear not,' said he, 'some changes will come,
When you're sixteen the job will be done.

Standing up tall, looking proud,
Tough as a bull, clever and loud.
Act as smooth as a dove,
Then you will find true love.

But for now you're small,
Facing a mirror on the wall.
Mini, ten years old,
The story still to be told.

Relax, enjoy and stay steady
Then the time will come and you'll be ready!'

Max Goreham (10)
The Daiglen School

The Devil

A harsh and cruel jailer,
A scavenger picking off the dead.
His fork as sharp as broken glass,
He's a black hole sucking up the evil.

James Wright (10)
The Daiglen School

My Hedgehog

My hedgehog is as slow as a snail
But as sharp as a pin
He comes out at night looking for light
But ends up being seen.

He rolls up in a ball of prickly spikes
Like a pineapple hanging from a tree
He chomps away like a squirrel nibbling
At a pea!

Eren Sadik (11)
The Daiglen School

Death

Death is red,
Like lightning,
Striking the heart.
It's like poison,
Running through your veins,
Killing everything in its way.
Death is your body rotting away over time.
It's Hell, far, far away.

Jaikaram Sandhu (11)
The Daiglen School

The Cyclops

The Cyclops with its one eye
It ate the bus
It crushed the car
It made everyone run so far

The Cyclops took the people to its lair
They screamed and shouted but he didn't care
It attacked the stables
And a baby in a cradle

Someone must stop this monstrosity
So a sorcerer came and said his philosophy
The Cyclops was banished
And all animals and people came back to life.

Garth Jones (9)
The Daiglen School

Elvis Presley

E lvis is the most famous rock 'n' roller.
L oads of people love his personality.
V ernon Presley was his dad.
I t would be truly awesome to be like him.
S ingers are green with envy.

P eople will always remember him.
R ightful king of rock 'n' roll.
E veryone loves his music.
S ome people believe he is still alive.
L oads of people wish he was here.
E lvis Presley maniacs go crazy about him.
Y ou would love to be like him, rich and famous.

Samuel Meah (10)
The Daiglen School

Football

F ouls all around
O pposition shout at the other team
O utside the ground fans cannot wait to get in
T ough defenders at the back
B all made of leather
A ll players wear boots and shin pads
L ose when you score fewer goals
L ook for a player to pass to.

Saurav Prabhakar (10)
The Daiglen School

The Bankside View

I see Cleopatra's Needle,
With its sphinxes side by side,
I can see London Routemasters,
Gliding by and by.
I see the magnificent building,
Of the Houses of Parliament.
In the distance I can sight
The Gherkin, St Paul's,
And One Canada Square, a tower of great height.

In Soho, Centre Point stands tall,
And way back in Bloomsbury,
I see the Telecom Tower, it now seems quite small.
I always look at this scene,
Every time I walk upon Queens Walk,
Because in my opinion,
This is a beautiful scene.

Harrison Jones (10)
The Daiglen School

Blue

Blue is the nice warm sky.
It is the sea going by.
The glorious doves in the wind.
It is the tasty candyfloss.

Blue is the cool ice.
It is the kite in the sky.
It is the nice wrapping paper.
It is my favourite sticky sweet.

Blue is the glue stick.
It is the colour of my pencil case.
It is the colour of my front door.
It makes me feel like fun.

Ryan Williams (8)
The Daiglen School

Snow

Snowflakes falling on my head,
Shivering cold and crumbly ice,
All the pine trees covered in white,
With sparkly icicles that store cold delight.
Snowballs are icy and cold
Twinkling brightly in my eyes,
Falling from my head to toe
It feels like I'm falling, *oh no!*

Zachary Cohen (8)
The Daiglen School

The Snowman

Children build me up with snow,
A carrot, a scarf, a hat and gloves.
Snow is powder just like me, feel me, touch me, in the snow.
Don't cry as I melt, I will come back next time.
Come and watch me twinkle in the stars as I melt.
Tomorrow build me up with snow so we can play once more.
Over the night I grow back into sight, as more snow falls.
This time build me up with a stone, 4 snowballs, a carrot,
A scarf and a hat.

Charlie Wright (8)
The Daiglen School

My Dog

She is a werewolf,
Always biting at Rolf,
She acts like global warming,
Always coming with no warning,
She looks like a black fog,
Trapping people in her bog,
She is a true pest,
I don't want to tell you the rest,
But here it goes,
She's got stinky toes.

Damien Zimelstern (11)
The Daiglen School

Snow

Snow, snow
Fast and slow,
What a happy way to go
Snow, snow
Fast and slow
What a happy way to go
Sliding on a sledge
Running on the snow
Sliding on the sledge
Running on the snow
Snow, snow
Fast and slow,
What a happy way to go.

Jasmine Samson (7)
Westborough Primary School

I Like Storms

I think storms are great.
The thunder crashes
The lightning flashes,
Storms are cool,
Storms are great,
Then it starts to rain
And if I don't get home soon
I'm going to get wet.

William Semple (8)
Westborough Primary School

Snow

Snow is very bright
But it doesn't show at night.

When I wake up I'm all excited so
I can have a snowball fight.

Every time it's night
You see the moonlight.

Because the snow is bright
You see it far out of sight.

Ashleigh Gill (8)
Westborough Primary School

The Slow Moving Turtle

A turtle crawls slowly over the white sand,
Its shell as hard as diamonds,
Its eyes are black as night,
As strong as a rhino's horn,
It's as fast as lightning when it's in water
As slow as an old woman walking as slowly as she can.

Jasper Huxtable (9)
Westborough Primary School

Snake

As green as a growing field
Growing as fierce as a leopard stalking its prey.
Snake as sly as a fox hunting for food
As quick as lightning hitting a road.
As strong as an elephant on its rampage
People cower as they hear its song.
Villages abound by its poisonous teeth
As cold ice is disguised in the tree as a vine.

Thomas Parker (9)
Westborough Primary School

Cat

Claws as sharp as a razor, cutting your hair
As furry as a fluffy lump of hair
Nose as wet as a river.
The tail swishing like the Union Flag.
His eyes green as a new patch of grass.
Sly as a leopard plotting to catch his prey.

Ben Crawford (10)
Westborough Primary School

Snake Over Head

Slimy like goo, as slippery as a snake sliding through the slippery sand.
As venomous as a scorpion, as scary as Dracula.
Climbs up trees as high as Redwoods as deadly as a bounty hunter, as slick as Rooney when he scores.
As quiet as a feather.

Thom Amar (10)
Westborough Primary School

Snake Surprise

Snake, what a shake you can't bake,
They slither through the dirt
As dirty as a footballer
Scaly as a dragon.
Thin as a stick
Python is a blood killer
You can't argue with that
Their teeth are as sharp as razor blades.
Would you like to touch one?
They love to eat pathetic little mice
Yum, yum, yum
In my big, fat, fat, fat belly.

Robin Tidd (10)
Westborough Primary School

Turtles

Turtles are heavy like a car.
Their shell is like a house.
They are as slow as a snail.
They are as boring as my brother.
They are as big as a rock.
They are as green as the grass.
They are as strong as Superman.
They swim like lightning in the water.

Daisy Appleton (9)
Westborough Primary School

Slithery Snake

I'm as slithery as a slug and I fidget all day long.
My bites are really venomous and I could be long or short
My body is as thin as a pencil and I can be poisonous.
Who am I?

Mollie Fryer (10)
Westborough Primary School

Snake

Tongue as long as the Great Wall of China
Fierce as a brave lion wandering through the forest
Scaly as a fish going round and round in his fishbowl
As long as the Siberian railway
As poisonous as a poisonous spider
Hisses at you in the long grass
Snakes are great!

Liam Davis (10)
Westborough Primary School

Cat

Whiskers as thin as wire,
Claws like razor blades,
Purring and licking himself all day long,
Likes fish as much as a lion likes meat,
As furry as a lion's mane,
As lazy as a sloth on a wet day.

Danielle Jefferies (9)
Westborough Primary School

Cat

Sly as a fox catching its prey.
Claws as sharp as razors.
Purrs as loud as a motorbike beaming along the road.
As furry as a polar bear on a cold winter's night.
Its colours may vary, they could come grey and hairy.
I could be ginger, black, white and brown.
I am a cat, please don't have a fright.

Rochana Reeves (9)
Westborough Primary School

My Cat

My cat is black and white,
But does not bite.
His teeth as sharp as a chef's knife.
Purring like a lion.
He likes to play with wool and is very small.
His nose is as wet as the River Thames on a rainy day.
His fur as soft as a rosebud.
He is as lazy as a tree when the wind isn't blowing.
He watches the fish leap up and down
And my hamster running around.
His ears are as pointy as a holly leaf.
He has great eyesight and is very bright.
That is my cat!

Alexia Parks (10)
Westborough Primary School

Beautiful Butterflies

Butterflies are beautiful,
So bright and full of colour
Their symmetry is amazing,
They're tickly on your arms,
Fast and thin, so special you grin
As fast as the wind,
On a stormy night,
So rare that if you see one,
They'll give you a fright!
Butterflies are as shy
As a mouse!
They're about two times the size of a woodlouse!

Sophia Shaw (9)
Westborough Primary School

Sunshine

The sun is hot and bright
But it doesn't show at night.
I wish I could see it every day
But some days it fades away.
I go out to play
And sun shines on me all day.
I wish the sun was mine
But there would be nothing left to shine.

Jessica Lynch (8)
Westborough Primary School

The Moon

The moon has a beautiful spherical shape
So beautiful that it will make you gape
The shimmering moon hides in the clouds
There's no sound but wolves' howls
The moon is in the sky, so high
But you cannot get to its height
All you can see is the moon's light
That's the greatest sight at midnight
The owl's eyes gleam
And the moonlight beams
The trees sway in the cold night's air
The wind passes through your hair
Silence is there when the moon appears
Whispering is all you can hear
The moonlight reflects on to your windows
The moonlight endlessly glows
The wind makes the doors creak
At night you should never play hide-and-seek
Or else you'll suddenly disappear
Have no fear, if the moon's here
Because it supplies a huge amount of light
The moon's the best helper at night
Beside the moon the stars twinkle
None of them have a single wrinkle
While the moon orbits the Earth, it visits all places
It greets everyone, and sees many faces
You want to get nearer and nearer
Then you can see the beauty of the moon clearer
It's a muddy banana in the sky
Way, way, way up high!

Eureka Zaman (11)
Westborough Primary School

Bike

There it is
Sitting in the shop
All alone
Getting rusty on its own
Slowly and sadly it won't be
Worth anything anymore
But when I save up
It will be healthy once more.

Maddie Davies (10)
Westborough Primary School

Timothy Winters

He is a poor boy
Lives in a dangerous place
Somebody help him
He shrivels all day and night
Somebody please . . . help him now
This is the poem of a boy
A boy named Timothy
But he is no more to see.

Chad Davies (11)
Westborough Primary School

Months

January jumps
February scuttles past
March is in the tub

April slips about the world
May, she hides nowhere at all
June discards his shirt

July by the sea, lazing
August by an emperor
September lies in shadows

October, apples on the tree
November's fireworks
December is Christmas time.

All year round is fun.

Isaac Smith (11)
Westborough Primary School

My Dad

My dad is wicked
He's the best in the world
I play football with him but I always beat him
He's got brown hair like me
I love him and he loves me
He's got ears like an elephant's
Eyes like a tiger
That's my dad.

Rhys Masterson (10)
Westborough Primary School

King

King of the jungle
Dangerous, shows lots of pride
Pouncing and jumping,
Sharp claws and big furry mane
The ferocious jungle king.

King of the jungle
Eating and ripping its prey
Sleeping all day long
Lions roaring very loud
The ferocious jungle king.

Lewis Sturley (11)
Westborough Primary School

The Wind

The wind is like a cheetah
Running through the wild
Any colour you want to think
We don't know
Can't see it
Never will
Never did.

Victoria Chinery (10)
Westborough Primary School

Wars

There are wars that can destroy homes,
Gunshots flying in the echoey shadow,
From Iraq to Africa wars over blood, diamonds,
Wars over Saddam Hussein and people with little power,
People falling to their knees because of gunshot wounds,
And death on their conscience.

Kieran Burns (11)
Westborough Primary School

My Mum

My mum is the loving one.
She likes everything neat and tidy.
She's got eyes like brown ice cream.
When all the work is done in the evenings
My mum becomes soft and cuddly
And I give her a hug!
She's a very peaceful person at all times
She is very humorous and very gentle
And I love her lots.

Amin Babar (10)
Westborough Primary School

Happy Animals

Hopping kangaroo
Jumping jackal
Birds flying around and around.
Three woodpeckers pecking
Two koala bears roaring
One soaring bird
Cheetahs cheating
Koala bears, beaten.

Klevin Demo (11)
Westborough Primary School

The Girl In The House

Once in a house there lived a girl,
Who was lonely and poor.
Her parents ran off a year ago,
Out of the garden door.

She has no friends,
She can't go to school.
Although it is quite near.
She won't leave the house, nor her room
Because she trembles with fear.

She has no food, neither a drink,
She's only skin and bone.
She never ever makes a noise,
No peep, a groan, or a moan.

No one knows this girl in the house,
No one knows her name.
But someone should help her now,
Or we will feel the shame.

Shannon Dorrington (11)
Westborough Primary School

My Day

On the horizon
Down below
Shining over people
Who don't know where to go
Busy everywhere
Shops all open
Hours go by
Shops all shut
Animals sleeping
Their eyes closed tight
Tired as midnight
Can't wait for morning.

Hannah-Louise Hill (11)
Westborough Primary School

Shipwrecked

He sits there all day long
Thinking of his family
Thinking of his home.
He's all alone
His only friend is his shadow.
He misses his family but they're all dead
He dares try to get back home.
The only picture in his head is death and destruction
And yet he's so calm.
When he finds a friend he treats him like a son
They hardly speak but they understand each other.
He has a chance to go home
He doesn't go
But he's not scared
He's happy where he is
And happy his son is going home to his family.

Rachel Ellis (10)
Westborough Primary School

WWE Poem

I love WWE,
I watch shows 'Smackdown' and 'RAW'.
They are really gore,
It entertains the fans too.
Batista is great,
He can't wait to be unleashed.
Dangerous matches
TLC, Hell in a Cell.
They put their lives on the line,
It's Batista time.
Undertaker, The Phenom
He's beaten them all.
The Phenom and Batista,
Rule WWE.
All the superstars are great.
But Undertaker and Batista are the best.
They are better than the rest.
That's why I love WWE.

Joe Hodges (11)
Westborough Primary School

Have You Ever Seen?

Have you ever seen a dancing cat
Or a little flapping bat?
Have you seen a jogging cheetah
Or even a building beater?

Have you ever seen a shopping frog
Or a weird looking talking dog?
Have you seen a rowing spider
Or even a sliding glider?

Have you ever seen a walking fish
Or a little reading dish?
Have you seen a tricycling chick
Or have you seen a moving brick?

Well, have you ever seen them?

Lucy Urquhart (10)
Westborough Primary School

I'm Going Away

I'm going away,
Time for us to separate,
The wind will take me,
I do feel so lonely,
Upset and sad,
My heart is beating too fast, too quick,
My brain is burning like a spinning top,
On the aeroplane,
I feel gutted, lost then found,
Shall I go to France?
The seaside is much better.
I think I'm going to go.

Raihan Uddin (11)
Westborough Primary School

Skipping

Up and down, yeh, yeh,
Jump over the rope or fall
All in a tangle
Help get me out of this stuff
Phew, no more skipping for me!

Jade Atkin (10)
Westborough Primary School

Red

Red is when I've eaten a pepper, tingling on my tongue.
Red is when I'm angry as a rhino
Red is joy, my heart skips a beat
Red is my favourite colour, top of the rainbow
Red is the reddest red rose on a rosebush
Red is a red, red nose on a winter's night
I love red.

Alex Fowler (11)
Westborough Primary School

Flexible Cats

Fast, flexible cats
Never wipe their feet on mats
Hunt at day, sleep at night
Tuck into their dinner with a violent bite
Lamb, beef, steak and maybe chips
That's their Sunday lunch, oh, and some dips
Little cubs playing fights
Mum and Dad by the glowing lights
Daddy spots a hare go by
While the cubs carry on playing and Mum just lies
Then the roar goes for children to go to bed
They've had their fun and been fed
So hush, hush, be calm, time for little ones to sleep.

Rebecca Cutmore (10)
Westborough Primary School

Untitled

I'll tell you something shall I,
Something I remember?
Something that still makes me cry
It was long ago
It was at home
I remember
My mum, my dad and my new baby sister
She smiled you know
Seven days of sunshine
I remember
But then it rained on the eighth day
So very sad
She was taken from us all
I remember
How she filled my
Heart with love
And care
So long ago.

Sophie Goddard (10)
Westborough Primary School

Mum

My mum is like a falcon
Vicious and cares for the family
But sometimes she is as soft as a puppy
Kind, gentle and loving
Sometimes she is both, I like her more as both
But mum is fine as a falcon.

Justin Davis (10)
Westborough Primary School

My Dog Max

I love my dog Max
He is so soft
Funny and fluffy
He is the colour of snow
Stupid and naughty but cute.

Victoria Johnson (10)
Westborough Primary School

Georgina

Georgina, Georgina you are the best.
Georgina, Georgina better than all the rest.
Georgina, Georgina you are my friend.
Georgina, Georgina our friendship will never end
Georgina, Georgina we will always be together
Georgina, Georgina forever and ever
Georgina, Georgina you make me laugh
Georgina, Georgina you're my other half.

Danielle Ford (11)
Westborough Primary School

Animal Sounds

Lions roar
Leopards leap
In the darkness in a heap.

Birds squawk
Bees buzz
Sometimes in a ball of fuzz

Dogs bark
Cats miaow
When they bite you scream 'Ow!'

Ellie-Marie Shuff (10)
Westborough Primary School

Snake

As deadly as a fully grown angry rhino.
As sneaky as a lion, stalking its prey.
As sharp as a freshly sharpened sword.
As smart as Einstein.
As slimy as a newborn without being cleaned.
As strong as a very fierce evil shark ripping a fish to pieces,
It slithers.

Maisie Davies (9)
Westborough Primary School

I Remember

I'll tell you something shall I, something I remember?
Something that makes me feel sad
When I fell off the roundabout only two years ago.
It was in the park
I remember
The grass and the children
And a boy
Who pushed my cousin
Onto my hand
I remember.

Jordan Chandler (10)
Westborough Primary School

Flower

Standing up straight
Like a bowl in the air
You smell like a perfume
You have a long tail
Which holds you facing the sky.

Anitta Abraham (10)
Westborough Primary School

Blue

Blue is like the ocean wave glowing like a tidal wave.
Blue is like the clear sky on a Sunday morning.
Blue is like a bird flying near the lonely sea.
Blue is the 7th colour of the rainbow in the sky.
Blue is like a shiny paper hanging on the wall.
I love blue.

Tasha Russell (10)
Westborough Primary School

The Jungle King

The king of the jungle,
The lion is he,
If I were to meet him,
I'm sure he'd eat me!
So I think it's best if I just stay away,
Maybe when I'm braver,
I'll see him in May!

Jack Whitehead (10)
Westborough Primary School

Offas Dyke

Last year I went hiking
With my dad in Wales
We walked 88 miles in total
Luckily, no rain or gales

We started off at Cheapstow
To walk Offas Dyke
I didn't get any blisters
And we didn't take a bike

We spent the day in Hay on Wye
My daddy bought lots of books
We posted them home
After having lots of looks

We hiked up the Black Mountains
And walked in the mist
It took us 18 miles
The clouds we nearly kissed

When we got to Newcastle
We travelled home by train
I felt very tired
But happy to see my family again.

Helena Layzell (11)
Westborough Primary School

About My Favourite Animals

My favourite animals pounce like cats
And they jump high in the air like two bats,
My animals run like Olympic winners
And they are always fitter than a cheetah.

My favourite animals are striped all over
And can never be run over,
They scare you in the middle of the night
And when you're in the jungle they will give you a fright.

Eunice Rutendo Mushonga (10)
Westborough Primary School

Young Writers Information

We hope you have enjoyed reading this book - and that you will continue to enjoy it in the coming years.

If you like reading and writing poetry drop us a line, or give us a call, and we'll send you a free information pack.

Alternatively if you would like to order further copies of this book or any of our other titles, then please give us a call or log onto our website at www.youngwriters.co.uk

Young Writers Information
Remus House
Coltsfoot Drive
Peterborough
PE2 9JX

(01733) 890066